GREAT YAI

and GORL_₋₋ı UN

The Floods - 1953

Colin Tooke

First Published 2002
By
Tookes Books
14 Hurrell Road
Caister-on-Sea
Great Yarmouth NR30 5XG

ISBN 0 9532953 5 4

Printed in England by Blackwell John Buckle
Charles Street, Great Yarmouth, Norfolk

Introduction

The year 1953 was, for most people in this country, a year to be remembered for joy and celebration. It was the year Elizabeth was crowned Queen Elizabeth II and also the year the world's highest mountain was conquered by a British-led expedition. For those living on the east coast of England however the year would be remembered for very different reasons, a year which would begin with disaster and great loss of life, for this was to be the year of the East Coast Floods.

The coastline of East Anglia is no stranger to storms, floods and gales during the winter months as on many occasions throughout the centuries there have been disasters both at sea and on land. The town of Great Yarmouth, low-lying and built on a sandbank, has always been vulnerable to flooding. Many parts of the town are only five feet above present day sea level and the highest part, Fullers Hill, is only twenty feet above sea level. The earliest record of a flood in the town is in 1287 when the parish church of St Nicholas was completely inundated by the sea which also caused much damage in the town, the greater part of which was under water. On 1 December 1557 the town was again flooded, men rowing up and down the streets and ships drawn over the Denes by windlass. Floods have also affected the surrounding area many times. In 1607 the sea broke through between Yarmouth and Happisburgh, flooding thousands of acres of farmland. On 1 February 1791 the tide was high enough in the town to enable boats to be rowed along the Southtown turnpike and on 3 February 1825 houses on the west side of this road were again flooded and considerable damage done in other parts of the town.

In 1855 one of the highest tides for many years was recorded. The wind blew hard from the north-west and there was a full moon, parts of Southtown were inundated as well as North Quay as far as Laughing Image Corner. The tide reached the north and south terraces on the beach and a large boat floated near the Holkham. Twelve years later Southtown Road and parts of the town near the river were again inundated, this time the banks of Breydon Water were breached. On 7 January 1905, again said to be the highest tide ever recorded, many parts of the town were flooded, one of the worst affected areas being Cobholm.

Southtown Road after the flood of 7 January 1905. A horse drawn tram is making its way through the flood water towards Gorleston. On the right is the Anson Arms public house, its original position being on the east side of Southtown Road.

These are only a few of the many recorded instances when the town and neighbouring countryside have been flooded by the sea. As well as suffering from flooding a lot of land along the East Anglian coastline has been completely lost to the sea, in many cases whole communities have disappeared at places such as Shipden and Dunwich. This erosion continues today. In the mid-nineteenth century, before any sea walls or the wide Marine Parade had been constructed, the sea often battered against the buildings facing the sea, many having their own sea defences in the form of low walls in front of the property.

It is inevitable therefore that severe flooding will occur at intervals along this coast, the town being no stranger to the wrath of the sea. The night of Saturday 31 January 1953 was exceptional, it brought to Britain's east coast one of the greatest peacetime disasters in history. Along the east coast, from Scotland to Kent, over 40,000 people were evacuated from their homes, over 300 people died and 150,000 acres of land were flooded. Many thousands of cattle, sheep, pigs and smaller animals were drowned. This was the night of the East Coast Floods.

Saturday

It was to be the night of a full moon and spring tide, the Meteorological Office at Dunstable issued a routine gale warning although abnormally low pressure was reported by the weather ships to have formed in the Atlantic. During the day the low pressure moved across the top of Scotland and into the North Sea, hurricane-force winds reached gusts of 125 mph leaving a trail of damage. In the Irish Sea a British Rail car ferry *Princess Victoria* was caught in the storm and overturned, resulting in 132 people, including all the women and children on board, being drowned. This was the greatest peacetime maritime disaster for 25 years and the story formed the lead item on the BBC radio news bulletins, not the unusual weather conditions. Weather reporting and forecasting at that time did not have the benefits of today's sophisticated satellites and computers.

As the low pressure moved into the North Sea it brought with it a surge of water which ran ahead of the high tide, taking about twelve hours to travel from Scotland down the east coast to the Thames. This surge of water was, in many places, to exceed ten feet and this in addition to the predicted height of the spring tide. By mid morning the Meteorological Office gave a warning to East Anglia of exceptionally strong winds over the North Sea but the situation was not considered too serious, gales in January were not unusual and this one gave no great cause for anxiety. By late afternoon however severe flooding had occurred along the Lincolnshire coast and in the absence of an official flood warning system it was left to the police to pass a telephone warning along the coast. The surge, whipped up by the high wind, was moving south with great force into the ever-increasing bottleneck of the southern North Sea, preceding the high tide by almost one hour.

As darkness fell on that Saturday night the people of Great Yarmouth treated it as a normal winter's night, the pubs were busy and many people had gone to the cinema or dance halls. The high tide was due at 10pm but two hours before this people crossing the Haven Bridge noticed the unusual height of the river. No official warning had been received but by 8.30pm a police loudspeaker car toured low lying areas near the river warning householders of impending flooding. People began to gather at the bridge and a short time later saw, what was described by the reporter for the Yarmouth Mercury as "a tremendous wave, like the bow wave of a fast ship curving away on either side of the granite bridge supports". Realising the severity of the situation the word quickly passed around the town, cinemas flashed warnings on their screens and many people began to make their way home. For some however it was already too late to reach their Cobholm homes, the raging waters from the river racing towards High Mill Road. By 8.45pm the sea had broken over the sea wall and flooded the Marine Parade and by 9pm the water had flooded many streets in Yarmouth, Gorleston, Southtown and Cobholm, and was still rising.

That night the sea attacked Great Yarmouth from three directions. Waves crashed over the sea walls from Jellicoe Road to the Harbour's Mouth while the river overflowed along its length sending water into many low lying areas of the town. Among the first to feel the full force of the flood were the inhabitants of Exmouth Road where within a few minutes houses were inundated to a depth of four feet. This water was soon to make its way to the southern end of Blackfriars Road.

Along North Quay the water rose through the drains until it was three feet deep in the area between the White Swan and the bridge. Many homes in Alderson Road were flooded with a foot of water, the water bubbling up through washbasins, lavatories and drains. By 10pm Lawn Avenue was under water as the River Bure overflowed, flooding the riverside allotments before pouring down Tar Works Road. The water reached a depth of three feet at the junction with Caister Road.

At 11pm news spread that the wall of Breydon Water had been breached in several places. These breaches caused millions of gallons of sea water to flow across the marshes into the town from the west, quickly turning roads in Southtown and Cobholm into swirling rivers. Men owning stock on the marshes immediately set out to try and rescue them. By now the town was almost surrounded by water and most lines of communication, both road and rail, had been cut.

Thousand of homes in the town were now inundated and rescue operations were under way. Where possible householders began to move furniture and belongings upstairs, a task made more difficult when the electricity began to fail and streets and houses were plunged into darkness. Southtown Road was partially illuminated when the Cross Sands lightship, moored at Bollard Quay, switched on its light. For hundreds of families it was to be a cold dark night spent upstairs, hoping for some relief the following day.

The Dutch Pier on the south side of the Harbour's Mouth suffered a considerable battering by the wind and sea at the height of the storm. At the end of the pier is the Coastguard Lookout where the coastguards were marooned for several hours. Gusts of up to 60 mph or near hurricane force were measured on the wind gauge at the height of the storm. The old pier was renewed in the 1960's.

Lichfield, Wolseley and Stafford roads were quickly cut off from the rest of the town, houses having four feet of water in the ground floor rooms. The water rushed into Southtown railway station, isolating it and leaving a signalman marooned in his box for the next 21 hours.

Along the sea front was a trail of devastation, shattered beach huts, chunks of sea wall torn out and large sections of the bathing pool wall smashed down. Gardens, bowling greens, putting greens and tennis courts were all under water to a depth of several feet. The Jetty shelters were almost destroyed and large sections of the Jetty itself ripped apart. The water reached the doorsteps of hotels and boarding houses on the west side of Marine Parade leaving a trail of damage and destruction. The manageress of Goode's Hotel said, "It was really frightening, at one time the waves were beating the front door". The Wellington Gardens were flooded and shelters on the south side of the gardens were completely destroyed. Near the harbour's mouth a section of the promenade was destroyed and the café damaged.

At Runham Vauxhall the public house stayed open all night. Many people had been marooned there including about 40 passengers from a train which had arrived at the station at the height of the storm. Although parts of the building were flooded the two front bars were dry and beer crates and wooden chairs were used to keep the fires alight during the night. The inhabitants of one low-lying bungalow in Runham Vauxhall spent the night on the roof, surrounded by six feet of water. The last train due into Vauxhall station had to terminate at Acle.

In parts of Gorleston it was a similar story. By 7.30pm the yacht pond was filled with seawater and by 9pm the seas were level with the breakwater. Soon Quay Road and other low-lying areas were three to four feet deep in water. At the Belle Vue public house the water rushed in and filled every room to a depth of four feet so suddenly that no one had time to leave before they were up to their waists in water. At the King William IV public house water rushed through the door and flooded rooms to a depth of six feet while the proprietor of the Pier Hotel said it seemed as if a tidal wave had swept through the building. At the Floral Hall (today the Ocean Room) the dance was ended at 10.30pm when the building was almost entirely surrounded by water. Many people were able to make their way to the safety of higher ground and continue dancing at the Cliff Hotel but others were marooned in the hall. These people had come by coach from outlying areas and had to wait several hours before their coaches could reach them via the Ravine and Lower Promenade.

At the prefabs on Bells Marsh Road the water rose well above the window sills but here the residents had no upper floor to retreat to and drowning became a real fear. In command of the Gorleston fire crew called to the area was Leading Fireman Frederick Sadd who lost no time in wading and swimming through the icy water to each prefab to find the rooms where people were trapped. By pushing a boat or carrying people on his shoulders Fireman Sadd led many people to safety even though at one time he collapsed with exhaustion, only to return after a short break. In one prefab he found a woman with two children on a bed which was floating about in the room, the occupants of the bed trying to hold on to the ceiling to keep it still. He managed to get them out through the window, carrying the family to safety. For his heroic efforts in saving many lives Fireman Sadd was later in the year awarded the George Medal by a newly crowned Queen Elizabeth II.

Along Southtown Road and South Quay parts of the road surface were made up of tarred wooden blocks and granite sets, many of these were lifted by the flood water making it difficult if not impossible for vehicles to make their way through, hampering the rescue work considerably. Later however these wooden blocks were to make a valuable addition to the free fuel available to householders to dry out their houses.

The first reception centre for evacuees was set up within hours of the disaster at the Gorleston Scout Hut. The Dene Side Methodist Hall was opened at 9pm and at Gorleston St Andrew's Hall (now demolished) in School Lane was opened at 11pm as the Council and emergency services swung into action. Appeals for clothing, blankets and food were made and many voluntary organisations including the Red Cross, Salvation Army and Women's Voluntary Service responded quickly to the disaster.

The remains of the Jetty after the seas had ripped up much of the wooden decking and destroyed the seating.

Early morning sightseers on Sunday 1 February looking at the damage to seating and fencing along the sea front done by the previous night's high seas.

The broken-down fencing to the Bathing Pool. Today this is the site of the Marina Centre, the pool being demolished in 1979.

The bandstand in the centre of the Wellington Pier south gardens
surrounded by sea water.

High Mill Road, Cobholm. Many chickens and domestic pets were rescued but hundreds were lost in this area.

Another scene in High Mill Road as livestock is brought to safety on Sunday morning.

10

The only access to the maltings which stood in High Mill Road was,
for several days, by boat.

A woman being taken to safety by canoe in Mill Road. Many different types
of boat were used to take people to dry ground, from where they were taken
to the rest centres.

Horses brought to safety from the Cobholm marshes. Several horses and ponies were drowned together with hundreds of pigs on the marshes before they could be rescued.

Bridge Road. In the background is the Two Bears Hotel where the main control point was set up to co-ordinate police and rescue services.

Vehicles from many local firms were brought into use for rescue work. The van is from Radio Relay, a wired radio system that operated in the town for several years from a main radio receiver in premises on Hall Quay.

The coaster *Raycreek*, one of the many ship that rode high at their moorings along the quayside. The present river wall was not constructed until several years after the floods.

One of the tall wood carriers from Jewson's woodyards taking people to
safety from the upper floor of their house where they had been stranded for
many hours. These Ross straddle carriers, which carried a stack of wood
slung below the vehicle, were at one time a common sight on Southtown
Road, moving large loads of wood between the different woodyards.
Throughout the 1950's and 1960's timber was one of the main imports
into the port of Great Yarmouth.

On Sunday morning many houses in Cobholm and Southtown received their
milk delivery by boat. In this case the boat has been brought from one
of the sea front boating lakes.

Stranded cars caused a problem in many streets, hampering rescue
work. Tractors and breakdown trucks worked throughout Sunday
to clear the roads.

One of the boats from the sea front Waterways in the Lichfield Road
area on Sunday 1 February.

Sunday

At first light on Sunday, a day that dawned bright and sunny, the town began to take steps to repair the damage and rescue those still marooned in their houses. In some areas the water level had gone down as the tide went out, leaving behind a layer of mud and filth. The Southtown and Cobholm areas however saw little change in water levels as the muddy Breydon water continued to pour through the breaches in the river wall. The Acle New Road was closed to all but essential traffic to allow rescue vehicles and relief supplies to reach the town as quickly as possible.

At 7am rescue work began at Gorleston when boats took people from upper floors of houses in Pier Gardens, Beach Road, Pier Road and Pavilion Road. Hot drinks, made at the Floral Hall, were taken to stranded householders. The boats unloaded their passengers at the foot of the White Lion steps and from here they were taken by bus to the various rest centres. All the low-lying land between the river, Baker Street and Blackwall Reach was flooded. Dock Tavern Lane was completely cut off.

Early on Sunday morning a Flood Relief Committee, headed by the mayor Alderman Barfield, was established at the Town Hall and from here the rescue operation was organised. A main control point was set up at the Two Bears Hotel and another at Calvers 'Seagull' Garage on Southtown Road.

During the day most of those stranded in the Exmouth Road and Blackfriars Road areas were evacuated to the Hospital School or homes of relatives.

About 9.30am two policemen arrived in Cobholm, the first contact the residents had had with the outside world since the previous evening. Rescue vehicles and boats soon followed and throughout the day people were taken to rest centres which included the Hospital School, Dene Side schoolroom, the Salvation Army Citadel and Rampart Road. Among the many rescue parties at work were the local Sea Scouts with their fleet of canoes. By the evening the rescue operation was hampered by lack of light and hundreds of people had no hope of rescue until the following day. The RAF had been requested to provide aerial flares but none were available. The early morning spirit of comradeship and hope, some people comparing it to the war time attitude during the Blitz, began to change when many people realised they were to spend a second cold, damp and hungry night in their dark and wet homes.

In Southtown it had been a similar story although here no rescue attempts were made until well into Sunday afternoon. High timber carriers from Jewson's woodyard, rowing boats from the seafront boating lakes and an army DUKW (an amphibious military vehicle) carried people to safety. The water level had been expected to fall during the day but the water from Breydon meant the ebb tide had little effect.

Servicemen were drafted in from the RAF, USAF, Army and Territorial Units to help with evacuation and rescue work. To prevent looting, extra police were brought in from Norwich and military police were also on duty.

Throughout the day animals were brought in from the Cobholm marshes to safety but many had perished the previous night as the water rose. Most horses and ponies were saved but hundreds of pigs and chickens were lost together with many domestic pets.

North Quay. On the left is the corner of the White Swan public house and the gate through which the railway passed onto the quay. The buildings on the right were part of Rainbow Corner, demolished in the early 1970's and now the site of the Post Office sorting office.

North Quay. On the left is the temporary bridge, opened only two weeks before the floods as a replacement for the old Suspension bridge, to carry the traffic across the river to the Acle New Road. The present bridge was not built to replace this 'temporary' bridge until 1972.

North Quay looking towards Fullers Hill and St Andrews church and school which was demolished in 1964.

The junction of Lawn Avenue and Caister Road. Water overflowing from the River Bure flooded this part of the town.

A typical Sunday morning scene in the Southtown area. The weather was bright and sunny, a complete contrast to the previous day's gales and storms. In almost every road boats were to be found bringing help to stranded householders.

Two views of Southtown railway station where normal services were not restored until 18 February. At this time Southtown was the principal station for the Yarmouth to London Liverpool Street services with eleven trains daily over the East Suffolk line via Beccles and Ipswich. The station closed in 1970 and was demolished in 1977.

Southtown Road showing the wood blocks lifted from the road surface by the flood water. These blocks later became a valuable source of free fuel for drying out houses.

The junction of Albany Road and Wolseley Road, one of the worst affected areas in Southtown. Houses here were flooded to an average depth of four feet. When the water subsided it left behind layers of mud and other debris which had to be cleared out before the long process of drying out could begin. For many years the flood water level could be seen on internal walls where the salt had penetrated the plaster, making redecoration difficult

As boats reached the higher end of the streets passengers had to be
carried the final few yards to dry land.

A lone policeman rows his way down Blackfriars Road.

The flood water reached half way along Blackfriars Road. Here a group of
Sunday morning spectators discuss the situation. The tower of the town wall
can be seen in the background. All the buildings seen in this picture were
demolished in a 1970's improvement scheme.

The occupants of 56 Blackfriars Road being helped into a boat by police and other rescue workers on Sunday morning. The general store of George Moore is on the corner of Louise Road. These buildings on the east side of Blackfriars Road have since been replaced by modern housing.

This picture was taken from the window of Bert Gibbs, the butcher, 49 Blackfriars Road. Where the buildings on the right stand is now an open space against the town wall.

Blackfriars Road. In this part of the town hundreds of fish barrels and boxes were washed into the streets from the fishwarf area. Here the boxes find a use as a temporary road crossing.

Sandbags being filled from the beach at the rear of the Marina open air theatre.

The prefabs off Bells Marsh Road, Gorleston, which were flooded to a depth
of several feet leaving the residents no escape route.

Leading Fireman Fred Sadd of the Gorleston sub-station. When called to the prefabs for a fire his crew discovered the flood and people calling out for help. The firemen started wading through the icy water but as it deepened Sadd, who was the tallest, sent the others back and went on alone, pulling a boat. He found people on top of cupboards and beds, rescuing some and reassuring others. By the end of the night, having once collapsed through exhaustion, Sadd had saved 27 people, a deed for which he was later awarded the George Medal.

This picture was taken at 7.30am on Sunday 1 February at the bottom of the White Lion steps, looking down Pier Road, Gorleston.

Rescued families being landed at the steps leading from Beach Road to Cliff Hill. On the right is a flooded Pop's Meadow. Howell's provision shop is today the Piccolo restaurant.

The shops on Quay Road to the north of the lighthouse. This shop is now
called Lighthouse News. In the background is the Harbour Hotel.

The King William IV public house, Quay Road, surrounded by water.

Clearing Up

At midday on Monday a general evacuation of the Cobholm area was ordered by the Town Hall but it was difficult to persuade many people to leave their homes, even after spending 36 hours marooned. Hundreds of people were taken by Corporation bus to the holiday camp at Caister while 150 were cared for at Gorleston St Andrews Hall and others at the Wroughton Junior School. The last people were rescued from Cobholm as night fell. Similar work continued in the Southtown area where it was reported that one man and his son rescued 85 people in six hours using a small paddle boat brought from a sea front boating lake.

From breakfast time a feeding centre was set up at Rampart Road by the school meals service. By 6pm Tuesday this centre had supplied 17,391 main meals, 37,687 sandwiches and 74,318 cups of tea. The Salvation Army and the WVS distributed the food and drink to both rescue workers and flood victims. The school meals supervisor, Mrs Elizabeth Mills, had opened the kitchen single handed on the first night of the flood and for her work throughout the week was eventually awarded the British Empire Medal. Later in the day 2000 blankets arrived in the town from Cambridge followed by 1000 from Southend. Large quantities of clothing arrived but some, such as six tons of women's overcoats, was not quite what was required. Three cases of whisky were received and these were distributed to the men working on the Breydon defences. By now more servicemen had arrived, including some from the Canadian Air Force, bringing with them specialised equipment including bomber-heaters from RAF Coningsby near Boston. Two lorries arrived from Ingham with 15,000 sandbags.

On Tuesday the Gorleston Holiday Camp was opened for refugees. The work of plugging the railway embankment was under way and a special train left Beach station carrying brick rubble, sandbags and workmen from the local building firm of H A Holmes. Work continued until midnight, by which time all the main breaches had been filled. Work on the wall continued the next day and for many days after.

Pumping began on Tuesday and fire pumps, together with the pumping stations on the marshes that were still working, were able to reduce the water level in Cobholm by 6 inches. The following day fifteen fire pumps and 70 firemen arrived from the Midlands to help pump the water back into the river and by Saturday many parts of

Southtown and Cobholm were almost dry. The Midlands firemen returned home on the following Monday and a team with 25 pumps from the London fire brigade took over.

Most children had returned to school by Tuesday although some had to be found places away from the flooded areas as four schools remained closed. Another gale and high tide warning was given for Wednesday evening but the night passed without any serious flooding. On Wednesday the RSPCA opened the stables at the racecourse as a reception centre for domestic pets rescued from flooded areas. The War Office had loaned the Society a DUKW from Taunton to help with the rescue of livestock.

On Thursday people were able to return to homes in the Bells Marsh and Dock Tavern areas of Gorleston. Notice boards at the Town Hall now carried lists of evacuated families and their new location. Long queues built up as blankets and clothing were issued, the main requirement being for children's clothes and shoes as most had been in bed when the disaster struck and they were rescued in their nightwear, their other clothes lost in the water. Within a week two disaster funds had been set up, a national appeal fund set up by the Lord Mayor of London and the Norfolk Flood Relief Fund set up by Sir Edmund Bacon, Lord Lieutenant of Norfolk.

By Monday 9 February all areas of the town were free of water and the Town Hall strongly advised householders to return to their homes to begin cleaning and drying them. They would advise people when their gas and electricity would be available but in the meantime fuel in the form of coal and wooden blocks from damaged roads was distributed. At Caister Camp there were still 363 people and at Gorleston Camp 130. A survey had shown that no houses were in danger of collapse and six sanitary inspectors began to make cursory examinations of all flooded houses and where necessary issue free deodorant and disinfectant. The receding water had left large quantities of mud and slime. By 20 February it was decided to close the Gorleston Camp but 84 families were still housed at Caister Camp.

The impact of the floods on local industry was to be felt for several weeks. Mason and Campling's laundries were put out of action, as was the engineering works of Pertwee & Back Ltd. It was estimated that 400 small businesses had been affected including 50 grocers. Many of these would eventually receive some compensation, either from the national or local funds. Both the Yarmouth and Gorleston Gas Works were put out of action for a time but the Power Station in Southgates Road was able to keep working despite water entering parts of the building.

A total of 4300 houses needed their electricity supplies restored and a team of 300 engineers was brought in, many from the London area. It was to take three weeks to restore the supply to all the affected houses, many having to be rewired, new meters fitted and appliances dried out. To assist in drying out houses several large hot air blowers were provided by the RAF and once back in their houses people were given a free allocation of coal. Several houses however were to remain unfit for habitation for many weeks after the water had subsided. Palmers used the old Plaza Cinema in the Market Place to store flood damaged furniture until it could be restored.

Mrs. Clementine Churchill, wife of the Prime Minister, visited the town on 17 February. She was flown into Horsham St Faith airfield and from there travelled in the mayor's car to the town and a buffet lunch at the Town Hall. The official party then toured the affected areas and Mrs Churchill spoke to many flood victims before meeting members of the emergency and rescue services at a parade held at the Two Bears control point.

On Sunday 21 February 250 tons of coal, given by a group of Lancashire businessmen, arrived in the town by rail. One hundred men with a fleet of 33 lorries then distributed this free fuel.

In Yarmouth nine people had died as a result of the floods, six had drowned and three died of shock. The body of one of these victims, an elderly lady from Cobholm, was not found until early March. At the inquest a verdict of "Death by misadventure" was recorded in each case. Twenty people had needed hospital treatment for minor injuries.

A plan to meet the possibility of further flooding had been set up by the Council and this was officially known as Operation Tantalus. By the end of February a permanent scheme was under way to strengthen the Breydon Wall, work which was estimated to cost £134,000 and which was to continue for many weeks. In March the first interim payments under the Flood Relief Scheme were made as vouchers were given out to cover the cost of furniture, floor covering and essential household items. Pensioners who had lost their Tobacco Tokens were allowed to apply at Post Offices for replacements. A team of assessors worked until July and claims for compensation from both householders and commercial firms continued to be met, these claims continuing throughout the year until by December there had been 4661 claims for a total of £450,618.

Following the floods the Publicity Department worked hard to deny rumours that the town would be unfit for holidaymakers in the coming season. The Council insisted that the sea front would be repaired or tidied up and fences and seating replaced. The Director of Entertainment and Publicity (Mr J Kinnersley) ordered a slight alteration to the wording of advertisements that were to appear in the national press. The slogan 'The resorts that have everything' would be changed to 'The resorts that still have everything'. Plans for the forthcoming Coronation celebrations in June continued and the town prepared for the 1953 summer season when stars of radio such as Jewel and Warris, Billy Cotton, Max Miller, Arthur English and the Five Smith Brothers would appear at the theatres.

Large hot air blowers were brought in by the RAF to assist with the difficult problem of drying out houses, particularly in Southtown and Cobholm. The problem of salt water penetration of the walls was to remain for several years, making redecoration difficult.

Looking down from Gorleston Cliff Hill to the gardens of Harbour Terrace with Pavilion Road in the background. After the flood water had subsided it was clear that considerable damage had been done to gardens and outbuildings. Almost all the buildings seen here to the right of the lighthouse and backing onto Pavilion Road have now been demolished.

Many back gardens in Yarmouth and Gorleston looked like this in the
aftermath of the floods, littered with debris and demolished walls

Following the 1953 floods millions of pounds were spent on coastal
defences and river walls in an effort to avoid a similar catastrophe. In
1976 another storm surge occurred, on Friday 2 January. By now a
flood warning system had been installed and this enabled vulnerable
areas to be evacuated in good time and there was no loss of life. On this
occasion the expected high tidal surge did not happen although at Great
Yarmouth the tide rose six feet above the predicted level, flooding being
averted by the new river walls. At Caister large sections of the sea wall
were damaged.

Only two years later, on 11 January 1978, a deep depression with
severe gales again caused a tidal surge, this one even greater than that
of 1953. Sea defences along the coast held firm and prevented serious
flooding although in many places the mountainous waves broke over
the top.

On 21 February 1993 the combination of high tide, gale force winds
and a surge once again hit the coastline. Many people were evacuated
but serious flooding was averted, the river overflowing only near the
White Swan. Nobody knows when the next North Sea surge will occur.

Local photographer D R Nobbs issued these multi-view
postcards following the 1953 floods. Today these are
sought-after collectors' items.

Acknowledgements

Many of the photographs used in this book were taken by local photographer Donald R Nobbs and are published here with permission of his grandson, to whom I am most grateful. Other photographs come from several sources including the collections of John Taylor, Peter Allard, Terry Ashbourne and Gordon Berry. To these I am also very grateful.

Every effort has been made to establish copyright for the images used in this book but in some cases this has proved impossible. Anyone with a copyright claim is asked to contact the publisher in writing.

The text has been researched from several sources including the Minutes of the Flood Emergency Committee, now in the Norfolk & Norwich Record Office (Y/TC 37/18) and the Yarmouth Mercury, various issues throughout 1953. Books consulted include *North Sea Surge* by Michael Pollard, published 1978 by Terence Dalton and *The Norfolk & Suffolk Weather Book* by Bob Ogley, published in 1993 by Froglets Publications.

To everyone who has encouraged the publication of this book, especially my wife Jan, I say thank you.